Summer Institute of Linguistics

**Language Data
Africa Series**

Publication 23

Pam Bendor-Samuel
Series Editor

William R. Merrifield
*Editor-in-chief
Academic Publications Coordinator*

Notes on Mada Phonology

Notes on Mada Phonology

Norman Price
Nigeria Bible Tranlation Trust
Jos, Nigeria

A Publication of
The Summer Institute of Linguistics, Inc.

Dallas

LANGUAGE DATA is a serial publication of the Summer Institute of Linguistics, Inc. The series is intended as an outlet for data-oriented papers authored by members of the Institute. All volumes are issued as microfiche editions, while certain selected volumes are also printed in off-set editions. A listing of available volumes will be sent upon request.

Copyright ©1989 by the Summer Institute of Linguistics, Inc.
Library of Congress Catalog No: 88-063673
ISBN: 0-88312-600-1
ISSN: 1040-4406

Printed in the United States of America
All Rights Reserved

No part of this publication may be reproduced, stored in a retrieval system, or transmitted in any form or by any means—electronic, mechanical, photocopy, recording, or otherwise—without the express permission of the Summer Institute of Linguistics, with the exception of brief excerpts in journal articles or reviews.

Copies of this and other publications of the Summer Institute of Linguistics may be obtained from

International Academic Bookstore
Summer Institute of Linguistics
7500 W. Camp Wisdom Rd.
Dallas, TX 75236

Contents

Introduction 1
1. The Syllable 3
2. The Interpretation of Segments 5
   2.1 Vocalic sequences 5
   2.2 Consonant plus sonorant 6
   2.3 Prenasalization 8
   2.4 Palatalization 9
   2.5 Labialization 10
   2.6 Consonant plus liquid 10
   2.7 Affricates 10
   2.8 Labial-velar approximant 11
   2.9 Labial-palatal approximants 11
   2.10 CN syllables 12
3. Structure of the Word 13
4. Tone 15
5. Phonemes 17
   5.1 Labial contrasts 17
   5.2 Alveolar contrasts 18
   5.3 Velar and labial-velar contrasts 19
   5.4 Contrasts with labialization 19
   5.5 Contrasts with palatalization 20
   5.6 Vocalic contrasts 22
6. Allophone Statements 31
7. Mada Orthography 35
8. A Mada text 37
9. The Swadesh 100-Word List 43
10. A dialect comparison of one-syllable word . . .45
References 49

Introduction

Data for this report were gathered under the auspices of the Nigeria Bible Translation Trust (NBTT), Jos, Nigeria. The author has been employed by NBTT since 1982, and has been serving as an advisor to the Mada Bible translation project.

The Mada language is classified as Benue Congo, Plateau IV, by Greenberg (1963) and Williamson (1971). In a more recent classification by Hoffmann (1976), it is listed as Benue-Congo: Eastern Plateau. The number of speakers has been estimated to exceed 30,000 (Grimes 1988). The people live mainly in the Akwanga and Keffi Districts of Plateau State and the Jema'a District of Kaduna State. Figure 1 presents a map of Mada villages. The names of villages included in the dialect comparison, in §10, are in bold face type in Figure 1. Villages in parentheses are not within Mada traditional lands.

The data for this report are based on the language as it is spoken in the village of Rija, which is located six kilometers west of Andaha, Plateau State. Although a more detailed camparison of the dialects of Mada is anticipated, the available data seem to indicate that Rija speech is representative of a dialect area which extends eastwards from around Ancho to around Numa and Buhar, and southwards from around Macu to, but not including Akwanga.

Another major dialect group lies to the east and northeast, including the villages of Ungwan Zaria and Anjida. Other dialects are spoken to the south around Akwanga, to the east of Andaha and Numa, and to the north of Andaha to Nunku.

The comparison of one-syllable words in §10 of this report is an attempt to show how far an orthography based on Rija speech will represent the speech of other Mada villages.

Figure 1. Map of some Mada villages.

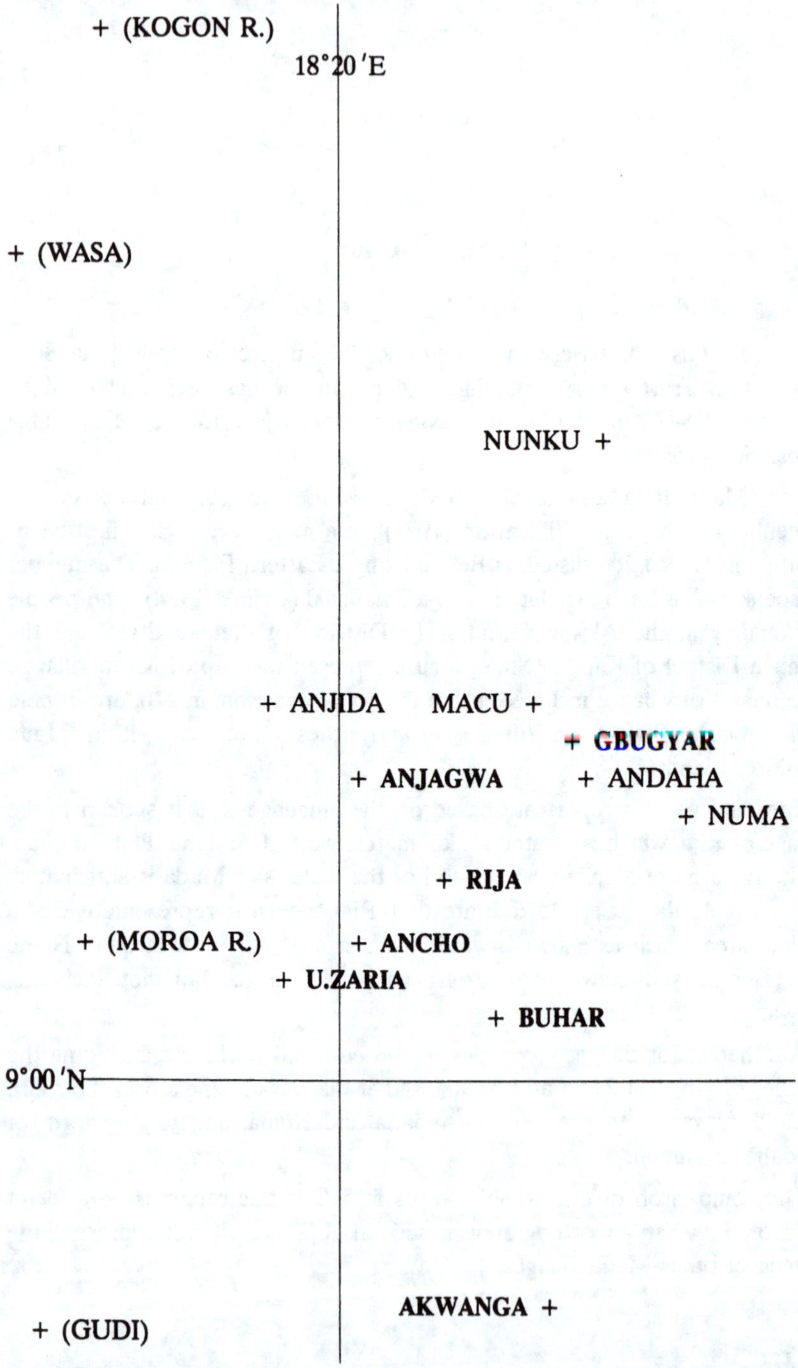

```
            + (KOGON R.)
                      18°20'E



+ (WASA)




                                NUNKU +




                    + ANJIDA    MACU +
                                       + GBUGYAR
                        + ANJAGWA    + ANDAHA
                                           + NUMA

                            + RIJA
         + (MOROA R.)   + ANCHO
                    + U.ZARIA
                              + BUHAR
9°00'N─────────────────────────────────────

                          AKWANGA +
  + (GUDI)
```

1
The Syllable

The syllable in Mada is the unit of tone placement. It consists of a nuclear, tone-bearing element with optional preceding and following marginal elements. The nucleus is normally a vowel, but in restricted environments may be a syllabic nasal. Syllable margins are consonantal. There are four syllable types in Mada—v, cv, cvc, and cn.

v	/ə/	'at'
	/ą.rį̄/	'because'[1]
cv	/kì/	'thing'
	/dɔ/	'to farm'
cvc	/tār /	'room'
	/dər/	'heart'
cn	/kpm̃/	'kapok tree'
	/gbm̃/	'canoe'

[ər] 'four days hence' is the only known example of a vc syllable pattern. Since /r/ otherwise occurs before every Mada vowel phoneme except /ə/, however, and since /ə/ otherwise occurs word-finally after every Mada consonant phoneme except /r/, the syllable [ər] is interpreted as /rə/.

The v syllable type, which is always either /ə/ or /ą/, only occurs word-initially and only in a very few grammatical function words, such as the following:

---

[1]Vowels marked with a cedilla are nasalized. See Figures 5 and 6 for an explanation of other symbols used in these notes.

/ə/   'at'
/a̰.r̰ɨ̰/   'because'
/a̰.r̰ɛ̰̀/   'before'
/a̰/   'and'

The cv syllable is by far the most common. Its margin may be any consonant and its nucleus any vowel.

The cvc-syllable nucleus may only be one of the vowels /a ə u/. The syllable-initial margin may be any consonant except /l r/, or any consonant modified by a following liquid [l r]. The syllable-final consonant may only be /r/.

The onset consonant of cn syllables is restricted to a labial-velar plosive /kp gb/. The nucleus is a homorganic nasal, arbitrarily interpreted as /m/ since labial-velar /ŋm/ does not occur in Mada.

2
The Interpretation of Segments

Mada presents a number of phonetically complex sequences which require interpretation as to their status within the syllable structure. These sequences are discussed in the following subsections. Figures 2 and 3, which present the vocoids and contoids of Mada, respectively, will serve to inform the discussion.

Figure 2. Phonetic chart of vocoids

```
ORAL                          NASAL
i      ɨ   ʉ   u              į               ų
  ɪ                             į̞
eʸ     ə       o              ęʸ              ǫ
ɛ              ɔ              ɛ̨               ɔ̨
   aʸ                            ąʸ
     a                            ą
```

2.1. Vocalic sequences. The only vocalic sequences which occur in Mada syllables have [w] or [y] as the first element or [y] following [a] or [e].

(1) [wV]   [wĩ]   'you'
(2) [yV]   [yè]   'it'
(3) [CwV]   [bwã]   'to fly'
(4) [CyV]   [kyɛ̨]   'to look'
(5) [Cay]   [bay]   'a monkey'
(6) [Cey]   [bey]   'yard'

The vocalic segments [w] and [y] do not carry a separate tone in any of the above occurrences. Illustrations (1) and (2) fit the normal cv syllable

5

pattern of the language. The glides in (3) and (4) can be interpreted as features of labialization and palatalization on the preceding consonants. The sequence [ay] in (5) is an allophone of /ɛ/, and [ey], as in 6, is always the phonetic realization of /e/.[2] For these reasons, no phonemic vowel sequences are recognised as occurring in Mada.

Figure 3. Phonetic chart of contoids

```
p    t        c    k    kp         ᴺp   ᴺt   ᴺc   ᴺk   ᴺkp
b    d        ɟ    g    gb         ᴺb   ᴺd   ᴺɟ   ᴺg   ᴺgb
m    n        ɲ    ŋ                                  
     ts   tʃ                            ᴺts  ᴺtʃ
     dz   dʒ                            ᴺdz  ᴺdʒ
f    s    ʃ                        ᴺf
v    z                             ᴺv
     l                                  
     ɾ                                  
     r    ʈ                        ᴺʎ
                     ʍ    ɥ
              y      w    ɥ
```

```
pʷ            kʷ                   pʸ   tʸ        kʸ   kpʸ
bʷ            gʷ                   bʸ             gʸ   gbʸ
mʷ       ɲʷŋʷ
    tsʷ tʃʷ
    dzʷ dʒʷ
    sʷ
    lʷ   ᴺʎʷ                                 ʈʸ
```

```
pˡ            kˡ   kpˡ             pʳ             kʳ
bˡ            gˡ   gbˡ             bʳ             gʳ   gbʳ
mˡ                ŋˡ               mʳ             ŋʳ
fˡ                                 fʳ
                                   vʳ
```

2.2. Consonant plus sonorant. In Mada the sequences of consonant plus sonorant which may commonly occur in the syllable onset are C[y],

---

[2]The phonetic notation for /e/ is simplified throughout this study to [e] except in the allophone statements (§6).

Mada Phonology

C[w], C[r], C[l], and NC, where [r l] are in complementary distribution and N is a nontone-bearing, homorganic nasal.

Since /y w r l m n ŋ/ are phonemes in Mada, all the sequences in question could be interpreted as sequences of two phonemes. In sequences of a nasal and a liquid, however, the elements of the sequence seem to have a different status than in other environments. The nasal consonants are not homorganic, as in other sequences, but contrast.

[mla]   to laugh   [mre]   to swallow
[ŋla]   to wash   [ŋrã^y] to see

The liquids /r l/, on the other hand, are not contrastive when in sequence with another consonant. In sequences of consonant plus liquid, for example, [Cr] occurs before front and high vowels, while [Cl] occurs before nonfront and nonhigh vowels.

with [Cr]   i   u
sequences   e   ə [ɩ]   o
              ɛ [a^y] a   ɔ   with [Cl] sequences

[krì]   yam   [klĩ]   hang
[krè]   to stand   [klã]   fry
[kra^y] finished   [klò]   an antelope
[kru]   gather up   [mblɔ̃] a lizard

But in cv syllables [l] and [r] do contrast.

[là] to help   [ra] to dream
[lo] to weave   [ro] to be heavy

In sequences of nasal plus liquid, the nasal appears to be dominant. This contrasts with other sequences, where the nasal is always homorganic with the consonant which follows. Likewise liquids, although in complementary distribution when following a consonant, are in contrast with one another as the initial consonant of cv sequences.

Because of the differing status of nasals and liquids in these environments, they are interpreted here as features or modifications of other consonants when nondominant—that is, a nasal before a nonliquid or a liquid following a consonant.

It also seems convenient to consider, by analogy, that a glide in sequence with another consonant in a syllable-onset margin is a feature of that consonant.

A simple consonant in Mada may thus be modified by features of prenasalization, palatalization, labialization, or by a liquid. These features are addressed in the following four subsections.

2.3. Prenasalization. Nasal segments commonly occur at the same points of articulation as a following nonnasal consonant. These nasal segments carry pitch, but the pitch is predictable, always being the same as the tone (or conclusion of the tone glide) of the preceding syllable or, if utterance-initial, being the same as that of the syllable nucleus which follows. Mada speaker reaction never seems to indicate that this nasal segment is preceived as syllabic. When whistling the tone of an utterance, for example, no place is given for such a prenasal segment.

The consonant phonemes which are known to occur with prenasalization are /p b f v t d ts dz l k g kp gb/.

p	[ᵐpā]	'a sore'	dz	[ⁿdzē]	'hiccough'
b	[ᵐbī]	'woman'	l	[ɲʎaʸ]	'four'
f	[ᵐfɩ]	'lungs'	k	[ŋka]	'four days hence'
v	[ᵐvaʸ]	'already'	g	[ŋgā]	'ladder'
t	[ⁿtàʸ]	'kidney'	kp	[ŋᵐkpā]	'time'
d	[ⁿdʉ]	'work'	gb	[ŋᵐgbɔ̀]	'swamp'
ts	[ⁿtsāʸ]	'star'			

In a multisyllabic word, a nasal consonant may occur word-medially following a vowel and preceding another consonant. In this context, the question arises as to whether the nasal belongs to the syllable which precedes it or to the syllable which follows.

[ncancù]   'a story'
[lūŋku]   'senior'
[tʃɩ̄ɲdʒi]   'a drum'

Of the nasal consonants, only [n] may occur in a syllable-final position at the end of a word, and that only after the vowel phoneme /ə/. A word-medial nasal which precedes a consonant is, therefore, normally interpreted as a prenasal feature of the consonant which follows. Only in the case of [n] following [ə] is there ambiguity, allowing the alternate interpretation, as in the following example.

[də̀ntswe] 'middle'

Prenasalization is grammatically restricted, in that it occurs only rarely in verb roots (see discussion of [ʎ] in §2.4).

2.4. Palatalization. The consonant phonemes which may occur with a feature of palatalization are /p b t r kp gb ʍ/.

p^y	[pyī]	'shoulder'	kp^y	[vīkp^{y}īr]	'duiker'
b^y	[b^{y}ι]	'rotten'	gb^y	[gb^{y}ɛ]	'straight razor'
t^y	[t^{y}ī]	'rusted'	ʍ^y	[ɥī]	'a fish' (§2.9)
r^y	[ŋ^{m}gbɛɾ^{y}ą̀]	'fish'			

Palatalization is not heard preceding back vowels, but the pairs [c k^y] and [ɟ g^y] occur in complementary distribution. The palatal sounds [c ɟ] occur preceding back vowels, whereas the palatalized [k^y g^y] occur preceding nonback vowels. Since these palatal and palatalized sounds contrast with velar and alveolar stops of corresponding voicelessness and voicing, palatalization is considered to be a feature, both in the case of palatal and palatalized allophones.

k^y	[k^{y}ɛ]	'to look at'	g^y	[g^{y}àr]	'bush cow'
	[cu]	'to die'		[ɟɔ]	'to call'

In addition to the above palatalized consonants, the palatal forms [ɲ tʃ dʒ ʃ] are also interpreted to be the palatalized counterparts of velar nasal and alveolar nonstop, nonnasal consonant phonemes.

ŋ^y	[ɲą̀]	'horse'	dz^y	[dʒų̄]	'to remove'
ts^y	[tʃī]	'rat'	s^y	[ʃɔ̄]	'bee'

Palatal [ʎ] also occurs, but not without prenasalization. The identification of this sound as a true voiced palatal lateral approximant is not presented here as absolutely certain. It is articulated with the tongue front at the palate and with the tip of the tongue down behind the lower teeth. There seems to be a lateral release of air, but literate speakers of the language never write 'l' for this sound. Their intuition often fails them altogether on this, and I have yet to see anyone suggest that it should be written as 'l'.

Another unusual aspect of [ʎ] is that it only occurs prenasalized and only in two word forms in available known data.

[ⁿʎāʸ]   'four', 'lightning', 'to discipline'
[ⁿʎʷe]   'to kill (plural object)'

The definitions 'to discipline' and 'to kill' are inconsistent with prenasalization, however, in that verbs are never otherwise prenasalized. Nor does unpalatalized /l/ occur prenasalized elsewhere.

It is tempting to think that [ʎ] may be an allophone with [ɽʸ] of /dʸ/. All plosives occur with palatalization except [dʸ]. Furthermore, [ʎ ɽʸ] are in complementary distribution; [ʎ] occurs before front vowels, [ɽʸ] occurs elsewhere. [ʎ] may occur labialized, however, as in [ⁿʎʷe] 'to kill', but neither [t] nor [d] do. If [ʎ] were an allophone of /dʸ/, and /dʸʷ/ occurred, /tʷ/ and /dʷ/ would also be expected to occur.

Another inconsistency associated with [ʎ], as in the case of [ⁿʎāʸ], is that the expected allophone following [ʎ] should be [ɛ] and not [aʸ]. That is because [ɛ] and [aʸ] are allophones of /ɛ/, with [ɛ] occurring only after palatalized consonants and /y/.

2.5. Labialization. The consonant phonemes which are known to occur with a feature of labialization are /p b ts dz s l y k g ŋ/. Labialization is not contrastive before a rounded vowel.

pʷ	[pʷà]	'undeveloped, empty'	lʷ	[lʷẽ]	'garden egg'
bʷ	[bʷā]	'to fly'	yʷ	[ɥẽ]	'pumpkin'
tsʷ	[tsʷẽ]	'place'	kʷ	[kʷar]	'all'
dzʷ	[dzʷẽ]	'to follow'	gʷ	[gʷǎ]	'snake'
sʷ	[sʷẽ]	'to bathe'	ŋʷ	[ŋʷār]	'to filter'

2.6. Consonant plus liquid. The consonant phonemes which are known to occur with a liquid feature, here written as /Cʳ/ (recall from §2.2 that [Cʳ Cˡ] are in complementary distribution), are /p b m f v k g ŋ kp gb/.

pʳ	[pʳě]	'gruel'	kʳ	[kˡa]	'to pound earth'
bʳ	[bˡa]	'to teach'	gʳ	[gˡò]	'fire'
mʳ	[mʳě]	'to swallow'	ŋʳ	[ŋʳi̧]	'to give birth'
fʳ	[fʳẽ]	'to peel'	kpʳ	[kpˡa]	'unmarried'
vʳ	[vʳẽ]	'day after tomorrow'	gbʳ	[gbʳe]	'ripe'

2.7. Affricates. Four phonetic affricates [ts dz tʃ dʒ] occur in Mada; but since [tʃ dʒ] are interpreted as /tsʸ dzʸ/, respectively (§2.4), only [ts dz] are in question. These are interpreted here as unit phonemes /ts dz/.

Mada Phonology

Since [dz z] are allophones and since [ʒ] (/zʸ/) does not occur, Mada is here analysed as having no phoneme /z/; that is, both [dz z] are allophones of /dz/ and not of /z/.[3] The affricate [dz] is, therefore, not interpreted as a sequence of /d/ followed by /z/, but as a unit /dz/, and [ts] is also so interpreted, as /ts/, by analogy.

2.8. Labial-velar approximant. The voiceless labial-velar approximant [ʍ] may be interpreted as a simple consonant phoneme or voiceless glottal approximant [h] with the added feature of labialization. Since [h] never occurs before unrounded vowels without the feature of labialization (except in ideophones and borrowed words), the voiceless labial-velar approximant is interpreted as being a simple phoneme /ʍ/.

2.9. Labial-palatal approximants. The voiced labial-palatal approximant [ɥ] occurs with different vowel sounds than its voiceless counterpart [ɥ̊].

/e/	[ɥe]	'to go'
[aʸ]	[ɥāʸ]	'egg'
	[ɥàʸ]	'hippopotomus'
[ɛ]	[ɥ̊ɛ̰]	'to pluck fruit'

The vowel /e/ never occurs following a palatalized consonant or following a palatal consonant unless the palatal consonant is labialized.

The vowel /ɛ/ has two allophones [ɛ aʸ]. [aʸ] occurs with the same restriction as /e/. [ɛ], on the other hand, occurs only following palatalized consonants or unlabialized palatal consonants. Since [ɥ] occurs before /e/ and [aʸ], but never before [ɛ], it is interpreted as a labialized palatal approximant /yʷ/. However, [ɥ̊] does occur before [ɛ], but never before [aʸ] or /e/. [ɥ̊] is, therefore, interpreted as the palatalized labial-velar approximant /ʍʸ/.

The known distribution of features of palatalization (Y), labialization (W), liquid (R), and prenasalization (N) with other onset consonants is summarized in Figure 4.

---

[3]Two voiceless fricatives [f s] occur in Mada but only one voiced fricative [v]. While [f v] do contrast in certain environments (§5.1), there are others in which they do not seem to have separate phonemic status. The noun prefix morpheme [fə] 'small', for example, is sometimes [və] under what is probably a tonal influence.
[fə-ji] 'small mortar'
[fə-mbĩ] 'small woman'
[və-ɟɔ̰̃] 'small hare'

Figure 4. Distribution of onset consonants with secondary features

C	Cʸ	Cʷ	Cʸʷ	ᴺC	ᴺCʸ	ᴺCʷ	ᴺCʸʷ	Cʳ	ᴺCʳ
p	pʸ	pʷ		ᴺp		ᴺpʷ		pʳ	ᴺpʳ
b	bʸ	bʷ		ᴺb		ᴺbʷ		bʳ	
m								mʳ	
f				ᴺf				fʳ	
v				ᴺv				vʳ	ᴺvʳ
t	tʸ			ᴺt					
d				ᴺd					
n									
ts	tsʸ	tsʷ	tsʸʷ	ᴺts	ᴺtsʸ		ᴺtsʸʷ		
dz	dzʸ	dzʷ	dzʸʷ	ᴺdz	ᴺdzʸ		ᴺdzʸʷ		
s	sʸ	sʷ							
r									
l		lʷ			ᴺlʸ		ᴺlʸʷ		
y		yʷ							
k	kʸ	kʷ		ᴺk				kʳ	
g	gʸ	gʷ	gʸʷ	ᴺg		ᴺgʷ		gʳ	
ŋ	ŋʸ	ŋʷ	ŋʸʷ					ŋʳ	
kp	kpʸ			ᴺkp				kpʳ	
gb	gbʸ			ᴺgb				gbʳ	ᴺgbʳ
ʍ	ʍʸ								
w									

2.10. CN syllables. Syllables occurring without any oral release occur with both labial-velar and velar plosives in syllable onset position.

[kpŋm̃]   'kapok tree'
[gbŋm̃]   'canoe'
[kpa.kŋ.kì]   'tree stump'

The onset of the nasal release [ŋ] is voiceless following voiceless consonants [kp k]. [kpŋm gbŋm] occur only word finally, whereas [kŋ] only occurs nonfinally. Since there are few examples of syllables with no oral release, comparisons are difficult to make. [kŋ] is tentatively being interpreted as /kpm/. The nasal release is, of course, homorganic; but since /ŋm/ does not occur as a separate phoneme, /m/ is here chosen arbitrarily.

3
Structure of the Word

No attempt is made here to define the phonological word in Mada. What follows is a brief description of grammatical words in terms of Mada syllable structure.

In a list of approximately 1000 words, 55% were found to have only one syllable, 39% two syllables, and 6% three syllables. There was only one four-syllable word in the list, borrowed from Hausa—pə̀làpələ 'oar', from Hausa filafili. Of the multisyllabic words, only about 1.5% were verbs.

As mentioned above (§1), the v syllable occurs only word initially, and only in a very few grammatical function words. The CN syllable occurs infrequently; a complete list of known examples is as follows:

/gbm̃/	'canoe'	/kpm̀/	'to plow'
/kpm/	'to fold'	/kā.gbm̃/	'to go home'
/kpm̃/	'to thresh'	/kpa.kpm.kì/	'tree bark'
/kpm̀/	'kapok tree'		

The cvc syllable occurs in word-initial, mid, and final positions.

/bǎr.ga/	'lion'
/də̄.dār.gʳō/	'rainbow'
/ᴺgbà.ᴺgbə̀r/	'navel'

cv syllables of any complexity occur in all positions of multisyllabic words.

/gbə.dzʸā/	'ugly'	/bə̄.bā.rī/	'butterfly'
/ᴺga.sʷe/	'twins'	/tsʸí.ᴺts ʸi/	'a fly'
/ʍʸu.ʍʸur/	'near'	/ᴺtsʸù.kù.rʸɔ́/	'pounded yam'
/mʷā.mʷăr/	'naked'	/də̀.ᴺtsʷe/	'middle'
/bʳĕ.kʳī̃/	'yam heap'		

4
Tone

These notes on Mada tone represent a stage of research which precedes insights from autosegmental phonology. Further study is already beginning to show that Mada has just three tones—high (unmarked), mid (¯), and low (`). But these data are here represented as having five, with rising (ˇ) and falling (ˆ) glides added to the three level tones. The falling tone is infrequent, never occurring on nouns, and, in fact, no single word class exhibits more than four tone contrasts. Verbs, in particular, may occur with high tone in some contexts and rising tone in others, but the two tones never contrast in the same environment. Rising tone is, therefore, interpreted here as a simple high tone on verbs. The five tones are illustrated as follows:

yèmē sē dzʸi	[_ _ _ ¯]	'this is a mortar'
yèmē sē mpɔ̄	[_ _ _ _]	'this is a calabash'
yèmē sē tsʸî	[_ _ _ _]	'this is a rat'
yèmē sē dǎ	[_ _ _ ╱]	'this is a cutlass'
ŋkɔ̀ sē yʷɛ	[_ _ ¯]	'the road is narrow'
ŋkɔ̀ sē hū	[_ _ _]	'the road is wide'
ŋkɔ̀ sē ŋgɔ̀	[_ _ _]	'the road is big'
ŋkɔ̀ sē ntsʸɔ̂	[_ _ ╲]	'the road is straight'
wɔ̄ là cu	[¯ _ ╱]	'you are dying'
wɔ̄ là sɔ̄	[¯ _ _]	'you are drinking'
wɔ̄ là sɔ̀	[¯ _ _]	'you are staying

There also appears to be a morphophonemic downstep feature (ˈ) which has been found in only one grammatical context, namely, when the third-person-singular pronoun *kə* is followed by the future-tense morpheme *lə*.

wɔ̄ lə sɔ̄ mɔ̀ [— ⁻ — _] 'you will drink wine'

kəˈlə sɔ̄ mɔ̀ [⁻ ⁻ — _] 'he will drink wine'

5
Phonemes

In this section, lexical material is assembled as evidence for the phonemic contrasts which exist in Mada. The consonant and vowel phonemes are presented in figures 5 and 6, respectively. Note that the following sets of vowel allophones [ɛ,aʸ], [ɛ̣ ạʸ], [ə ɪ ɨ], and [u ʉ] (See §6 for distributional statements in regard to these and other allophones) are treated as such for contrasting consonant phonemes in this section.

Figure 5. Mada consonants

		labial	alveolar	velar	labial-velar
STOP	vl	p	t	k	kp
	vd	b	d	g	gb
NASAL		m	n	ŋ	
AFFRICATE	vl		ts		
	vd		dz		
FRICATIVE	vl	f	s		
	vd	v			
TAP			r		
LATERAL			l		
APPROXIMANT	vl				ʍ
	vd		y		w

5.1. Labial contrasts. Labial consonants /p b m f v/ are considered to be in contrast because of the following examples.

p	b	m	f	v
[prẽ] gruel	[bẽ] outside	[mẽ] now	[frẽ] to peel	[vrẽ] 2 days hence
	[bă^y] monkey	[ma^y] to build	[fa^y] expose	[vą̃^y] child
[mpι] lid	[mbī] woman	[mì] beer	[mfι] hunger	
[mpā] sore	[bə̀bàṭì] butterfly	[mā] to meet	[far] to cut	[vàr] scatter
[pə̄mpą̄] tin can	[bą] take	[mą̀] to nurse		
[mpù] thigh	[mbŭ] jar	[mu] there	[fu] blow	[vʉ] carry away
[pwɔ́] eleven	[bwɔ̌] pocket	[mwɔ] kindle	[fɔ] to search	

5.2. Alveolar contrasts. Alveolar consonants /t d n ts dz s r l y/ are considered to be in contrast because of the following examples.

t	d	n	ts	dz
[tè] father	[dẽ] tiredness	[nẽ] people	[tsè] guinea fowl	[nzẽ] hiccup
[tī] we	[dī] to forget	[nι] to give	[tsī] pot	[zι] leg
[ta] throw	[dă] cutlass	[na] to do	[tsa] white	[zà] to jump
[tʉ] head	[ndʉ] work		[tsʉ] to die (pl)	[zʉ] bush pig
[to] pierce	[do] market	[nʉnʉ̀] somebody	[tsɔ̀] poison	[zo] to raise

Mada Phonology

s	r	l	y
[sē] to be	[ɾē] sharp		
[sɪ] to drink	[ɾɨɾē] long	[lɪ] sickness	
[sa] to be upon	[ɾà] baldness	[là] food	[yā] mother
[sʉ] cool	[ɾo] heavy	[lo] to weave	[yo] not
	[ɾʉ] come from	[lʉŋkū] senior	[yūr] he goat

5.3. Velar and labial-velar contrasts. Velar and labial-velar consonants /k g ŋ kp gb w/ are considered to be in contrast because of the following examples.

k	g	ŋ	kp	gb	w
[kì] thing	[gì] to cry			[gbì] to pull	
[kɪ̄] house	[gɪ̄] divide	[ŋɪ̀] rub	[kpɨkpɪ] cloud	[gbɨdʒā] wicked	[wɪ̄] you
[kà] crab	[gā] shoulder	[ŋā] break	[kpǎ] roof	[gbǎ] cock	
[kwɔ̌] bush fowl	[gwɔ] to hear	[ŋwɔ] arm	[kpɔ̌] bag	[ŋmgbɔ̀] swamp	[wɔ̄] blindness

5.4. Contrasts with labialization. Labialization of /b ts dz s l y k g ŋ tsʸ dzʸ gʸ ŋʸ/ is considered to be in contrast with these same consonants without labialization because of the following examples.

b	bʷ	ts	tsʷ	dz	dzʷ
[tɨbà] tobacco	[bwa] to pour	[tsē] clap	[tswē] place	[dzē] locust	[dzwē] to follow
[bɪ] they	[kɨbwɪ] yellow				

s	sʷ	l	lʷ	y	yʷ
[sē] to be	[sʉe] to bathe	[lɪ] sickness	[lwē] garden egg	[yē] it	[ɥē] pumpkin
		[nʌai] four	[nʌwē] to kill	[yã] mother	[ɥã] to cut

k	kʷ	g	gʷ	ŋ	ŋʷ
[kà] crab		[gã] shoulder	[gwǎ] snake	[ŋãɾ] to break	[ŋwãɾ] to filter
	[kwar] all	[gàr] army ant	[gwàr] din		

tsʸ	tsʸʷ	dzʸ	dzʸʷ	gʸ	gʸʷ
[tʃɛ] to grow	[tʃwē] full	[dʒì] to wait	[dʒʷi] to catch	[gyãr] anger	[ɟwãr] rush into

ɲʸ	nʸʷ				
[ɲĩ] elephant	[ɲwĩ] inside				
[ɲɛ] come	[ɲwɛ̣] children				

5.5. Contrasts with palatalization. Palatalization of /p b t ts dz s r l k g ŋ gb ʍ/ is considered to be in contrast with these same consonants without palatalization because of the following examples.

Mada Phonology

p	pʸ	b	bʸ	t	tʸ
[mpɩ] granary lid	[pyɩ̄] shoulder blade	[bɩ] they	[byɩ] decayed	[tɩ̄] we	[tyɩ̄] rusted

ts	tsʸ	dz	dzʸ	s	sʸ
[tsɩ̄] pot	[tʃɩ̄] leopard	[zɩ] leg	[dʒɩ̄] poverty	[sai] year	[ʃɛ] full
[tsãi] chest	[tʃɛ̄] to grow	[zʉ̀] bush pig	[dʒʉ̄dʒʉ̈] hole	[ʃʉ̄] cool	[sʉ] up
[tsa] gray	[tʃã] to learn			[sa] to be on	[ʃã] exist
[tsò] poison	[tʃō] to sew			[sɔ̀] straight	[ʃɔ̀] bee

r	rʸ	l	lʸ	k	kʸ
[ra] castrated goat	[ŋmgbɛ̄ɾyà] fish egg	[lwɛ̄] garden	[nʌwɛ̄] kill	[ku] dry	[cʉ̀] monitor
[rɔ] to play	[ryɔ] bush			[kwɔ̌] fowl	[cō] gather

g	gʸ	ŋ	ɲʸ	gb	gbʸ
[gɩ̀] divide	[gyɩ̄] you (pl)	[ŋã] break down	[ɲa] horse	{[gbi] pull	[gbyɛ]} razor
[gàr] army ant	[gyàr] bush cow	[ŋʉ] kill	[ɲʉ̈] mouth		
[gūgu] goat	[ŋgaɉʉ̈] dog	[ŋɩ̀] rub	[ɲɩ̃n] tooth		
[gwɔ] hear	[ɉɔ] call	[ŋwɔ] arm	[ɲo] odor		

ʍ	ʍʸ
[ʍɛ̰̃]	[ɥɛ̰̃]
salve	pluck

Figure 6. Mada vowels

	ORAL			NASAL		
	front	central	back	front	central	back
high	i		u	į		ų
mid	e	ə	o			
low	ɛ	a	ɔ	ɛ̰	a̰	ɔ̰

5.6. Vocalic contrasts. The vowel /i/, realized phonetically as [i], is considered to be in contrast with /e ə o ɛ a ɔ u į/ because of the following examples. Allophonic pairs [ɛ aʸ] and [u ʉ] are treated together.

i	e	i	ə	i	o
[ɥi]	[ɥē]	[kì]	[kɨ̀]	[ṭi]	[ɾo]
squeeze	go	thing	house	dirty	heavy
[ṭi]	[ɾē]	[ɥi]	[ɥɨ̀]	[tʃi]	[tʃō]
dirty	eat	squeeze	where?	rat	sew
[kṛ̀i]	[krɛ̀]	[gì]	[gɨ̀]	[ɲḭ]	[ɲo]
yam	stand	cry	divide	elephant	bad smell
[gi̯]	[gē]	[tʃi]	[tʃɨ̀]	[gbḭ]	[gbo]
to cry	or	rat	leopard	to pull	remove
		[dʒi]	[dʒɨ̀]		
		mortar	poverty		

Mada Phonology

i	ε	i	a	i	ɔ
[ɾi] dirty	[ɾaʸ] far	[ɥi] squeeze	[ɥa] cut	[kì] thing	[kwɔ̀] grind
[ɥi] squeeze	[ɥāʸ] egg	[ɾi] dirty	[ɾa] to dream	[gì] cry	[gwɔ] to hear
[kɾì] yam	[kɾaʸ] finish	[kì] thing	[kà] crab	[tʃì] rat	[tʃɔ̀] poke
[ɥī] a fish	[ɥɛ] narrow	[tʃì] rat	[tʃā] grain drink	[ɾi] dirty	[ɾɔ] to play
[tʃi] forehead	[tʃɛ] to grow	[gì] cry	[gā] shoulder	[ʃi] to peel	[ʃɔ̀] bee

i	u	i	i̠		
[ɾi] dirty	[ɾʉ] come from	[ɾi] sun	[ɾi̠] oath		
[tʃi] rat	[tʃʉ] pick out	[bɾi] ghost	[gbɾi̠] image		
[ʃī] to peel	[ʃʉ] up				
[kì] thing	[ku] dry				
[gì] cry	[ŋgù] feather				

The vowel /e/, realized phonetically as [e], is considered to be in contrast with /ə o ε a ɔ u/ because of the following examples. Allophonic pairs [ε aʸ] and [u ʉ] are treated together.

e	ə	e	o	e	u
[tè] father	[tɪ] we	[te] fetch	[to] pierce	[te] fetch	[tʉ] head
[tsē] slap	[tsɪ] pot	[ɾē] eat	[ɾo] to be heavy	[sē] to be	[sʉ] cool
[bē] outside	[bɪ] with	[tsè] guinea fowl	[tsò] poison	[nē] people	[nʉnʉ̀] somebody
[nzē] hiccough	[zɪ] leg	[nzē] hiccough	[dzǒ] raise	[bē] outside	[bū] darkness
[ɥē] go	[ɥɪ] where?	[dē] tiredness	[do] market	[gē] or	[ŋgù] feather

e	ɛ	e	ɔ	e	a
[ɾe] sharp	[ɾaʸ] far	[tsē] clap	[tsɔ] vomit	[ɥē] go	[ɥà] cut
[nē] river	[nāʸ] belly	[dē] tiredness	[dò] thorn tree	[dē] tiredness	[dǎ] cutlass
[ɥē] pumpkin	[ɥāʸ] egg	[tè] father	[tò] good	[te] fetch	[tā] throw
[bē] outside	[bǎʸ] monkey	[nzē] hiccough	[nzɔ̄] again	[tsē] slap	[tsa] gray
[tsē] slap	[tsāʸ] chest	[ɾē] eat	[ɾɔ̄] play	[ɾe] to name	[ɾa] baldness

The vowel /ɛ/, realized phonetically by the allophones [ɛ aʸ], is considered to be in contrast with /ə o a ɔ u ɛ̣/ because of the following examples. Allophonic pairs [ɛ aʸ], [ɛ̣ ạʸ], and [u ʉ] are treated together.

Mada Phonology 25

ɛ	ə	ɛ	o	ɛ	a
[ɥɛ]	[ɥī]	[ɾàʸ]	[ɾo]	[ʃɛ]	[ʃa]
narrow	where	sell	to be heavy	full	exist
[ʃɛ]	[ʃī]	[zàʸ]	[dzo]	[nè]	[nà]
full	carve	greet	raise	tick	horse
[gyɛ]	[gyī]	[ntāʸ]	[to]	[ɾàʸ]	[ɾa]
feces	you (pl)	saliva	pierce	sell	baldness
[tʃɛ]	[tʃī]	[gbyɛ]	[gbō]	[ntsāʸ]	[tsa]
to grow	leopard	razor	to marry	star	gray
[maʸ]	[mì]	[māʸ]	[mò]	[māʸ]	[ma]
build	beer	build	a lie	build	meet
[ntsaʸ]	[tsī]			[ɥāʸ]	[ɥà]
star	pot			egg	cut
[zàʸ]	[zɩ]				
greet	leg				
[ɥāʸ]	[ɥī]				
egg	where				
[saʸ]	[sī]				
year	drink				

ɛ	ɔ	ɛ	u	ɛ	ɛ̧
[māʸ] build	[mɔ̀] kindle	[saʸ] year	[sʉ] cold	[raʸ] far	[rą̄ʸ] speak
[saʸ] year	[sɔ̀] straight up	[ntāʸ] saliva	[tʉ] head	[ɥāʸ] egg	[ɥą̀ʸ] hippo
[ntsaʸ] star	[tsɔ] vomit	[ʃɛ] full	[ʃʉ̄] up	[ɰɛ] narrow	[ɰɛ̧] pluck fruit
[řāʸ] sell	[řɔ̄] to play	[ɲɛ̀] tick	[ɲʉ̀] mouth	[ʃɛ] full	[ʃɛ̧] wake
[ʃɛ] full	[ʃɔ̄] bee	[faʸ] expose	[fù] blow	[zàʸ] greet	[zą̀ʸ] winnow

The vowel /ə/, realized by allophones [ɩ ə], is considered to be in contrast with /a u o ɔ/ because of the following examples. The allophonic pair [u ʉ] is treated together.

Mada Phonology

ɘ	a	ɘ	u
[kɪ̄] house	[kà] crab	[mpɪ] cover	[mpù] thigh
[zɪ] leg	[zà] jump	[tɪ̄] we	[tʉ] head
[ŋgɪ̄] I	[ŋgà] section of house	[kɪ̄] house	[ku] dry
[gɪ̀] divide	[gā] shoulder	[mɪ̀] beer	[mʉ̄] that
[ŋɪ̀] rub	[ŋā] return	[sɪ̄] drink	[sʉ̀] pour
[tɘr] ghostly light	[tăr] room	[tɘr] ghostly light	[tur] push
[dɘ̆r] heart	[dar] lead (Pb)	[gyɪ̄] one	[gùr] ten
[sɘr] down	[sar] to cut	[sɘr] down	[sùr] boil
[gyɪ̄r] one	[gyàr] anger		

ə	o	ə	ɔ
[glɩ̀] monitor	[glō] rain	[tsɩ] pot	[tsɔ] vomit
[lɩ̄] sickness	[lō] to plait	[gɩ̀] divide	[gwɔ] hear
[tɩ̄] we	[tō] burn	[tɩ̄] we	[tɔ́] to be good
[mɩ̀] beer	[mò] a lie	[mɩ̀] beer	[mɔ̀] to kindle
[zɩ] leg	[zo] raise	[kɩ̄] house	[kwɔ̌] bush fowl

The vowel /a/, realized phonetically as [a], is considered to be in contrast with /u o ɔ a̧/ because of the following examples. The allophonic pair [u ʉ] is treated together.

a	u	a	o
[fā] cut	[fù] blow	[tʃā] learn	[tʃō] sew
[kpa] roof	[kpu] guinea corn	[gbǎ] cock	[gbō] lead away
[tā] throw	[tʉ] head	[tā] throw	[to] burn
[ʃā] exist	[ʃʉ] up	[dǎ] cutlass	[dō] market
[mpā] sore	[mpù] thigh	[zà] jump over	[zo] raise

Mada Phonology

a	ɔ	a	ą
[ra] baldness	[rɔ̃] play	[sa] to be upon	[są̃] ribs
[tsa] gray	[tsɔ] vomit	[lā] food	[lą] farm plot
[tʃā] learn	[tʃɔ̃] poke	[ɥà] cut	[ɥą̄] cover
[dǎ] cutlass	[dɔ̌] thorn tree	[ŋgā] pole	[ŋgą̀] many
[gwǎ] snake	[gwɔ] hear	[ma] meet	[mą̀] nurse

The vowel /u/, realized phonetically as [u ʉ], is considered to be in contrast with /o ɔ ʉ̨/ because of the following examples.

u	o	u	ɔ	u	ʉ̨
[ndʉ] work	[do] market	[ku] dry	[kwɔ̌] bush fowl	[tʃʉ] pick out	[tʃʉ̨] chief
[tʉ] head	[to] burn	[kpu] guinea corn	[kpɔ̌] bag	[tʉ] head	[tʉ̨] five
[tʃʉ] pick out	[tʃō] sew	[fù] blow	[fɔ̀] search	[dʒʉ̄dʒʉ̄] hole	[dʒʉ̨] to shed
[gbù] town	[gbō] to lead away	[ʃʉ] up	[ʃɔ̀] bee		
[zʉ̀] bush pig	[zo] raise	[tʃʉ] pick out	[tʃɔ̀] poke		

The vowels /o ɔ ʉ̨/ are considered to be in contrast because of the following examples.

o	ɔ	ǫ
[ro] to be heavy	[rɔ̄] to play	[rǭ] to ridge (farm)
[dō] sing	[dɔ̀] cultivate	[dǫ̀] shout
[tō] burn	[tɔ̀] good	[tǭ] ear
[tʃō] sew	[tʃɔ̀] poke	[tʃǫ̀] break
[mǫ̀] a lie	[mwɔ̀] to kindle	[mwǭ] more than

6
Allophone Statements

All Mada sounds are made with egressive lung air except as otherwise stated. All voiceless stops occur with aspiration.

/p/ [p] voiceless bilabial stop. /pàr/ [pàr] 'spear'

/b/ [b] voiced bilabial stop. /bū/ [bū] 'darkness'

/m/ [m] voiced bilabial nasal. /mə̀/ [mì] 'guinea corn wine'

/f/ [f] voiceless labiodental fricative. /fū/ [fū] 'liver'

/v/ [v] voiced labiodental fricative. /vṵ/ [vṵ] 'to seize'

/t/ [t] voiceless alveolar stop. /te/ [te] 'father'

/d/ [d] voiced alveolar stop. /dē/ [dē] 'tiredness'

/n/ [n] voiced alveolar nasal; occurs syllable initially and finally. /nē/ [nḛ] 'river'

/ts/ [ts] voiceless alveolar affricate. /tsə̄/ [tsī] 'pot'

/dz/ [dz] voiced alveolar affricate; in free fluctuation with [z] voiced alveolar central fricative. /zù/ [zʉ̀] [dzʉ̀] 'bush pig'

/s/ [s] voiceless alveolar central fricative. /sū/ [sʉ̄] 'to pour'

/r/ [ɽ] voiced alveopalatal flap; occurs before close-front and close-back vowels. /rì/ [ɽì] 'sun'

[ɾ] voiced alveolar tap; occurs elsewhere syllable initially, but occurs in free fluctuation with [r] syllable finally following /a/ or /u/, and in free fluctuation with [n] syllable finally following /ə/. /re/ [ɾe] 'sharp'

| | [r] | voiced alveolar trill; occurs in free fluctuation with [ɾ] in syllable final position following /a/ or /u/. /nār/ [nār] [nar̄] 'lightning' |
| | [n] | voiced alveolar nasal; occurs in free fluctuation with [ɾ] syllable finally following /ə/. /bər/ [bən] [bər] 'to appeal' |

Note: Before nasalized vowels [ɾ̃] and [r̃] are nasalized.

/l/	[l]	voiced alveolar lateral approximant. /là/ [là] 'to help'
/y/	[y]	voiced palatal central approximant. /yē/ [yē] 'it'
/k/	[k]	voiceless velar stop. /kì/ [kì] 'thing'
/g/	[g]	voiced velar stop. /gūgu/ [gūgu] 'goat'
/ŋ/	[ŋ]	voiced velar nasal. /ŋā/ [ŋā] 'to break down'
/kp/	[kp]	voiceless labial-velar stop. /kpu/ [kpu] 'guinea corn'
/gb/	[gb]	voiced labial-velar stop. /gbù/ [gbù] 'town'
/ʍ/	[ʍ]	voiceless labial-velar central approximant. /ʍə/ [ʍɩ] 'moon'
/w/	[w]	voiced labial-velar central approximant. /wù/ [wù] 'mosquito'
/i/	[ɩ]	voiced front unrounded vocoid between close and half-close; occurs word medially. /tsʸĩᴺdzʸi/ [tʃɩ̃ⁿdʒi] 'housefly'
	[i]	voiced close front unrounded vocoid; occurs elsewhere. /kì/ [kì] 'thing'
/ĩ/	[ĩ]	voiced nasalized close front unrounded vocoid. /dzʸĩ/ [dʒĩ] 'to wait'
/e/	[ẽʸ]	voiced nasalized half-close front unrounded vocoid with palatalized off-glide; occurs following nasal consonants. /nē/ [nẽʸ] 'people' ([sẽ] 'how?' is a single exception to the generalization that [ẽ] only occurs after a nasal consonant.)
	[eʸ]	voiced half-close front unrounded vocoid with palatalized off-glide; occurs elsewhere. /dē/ [dēʸ] 'tiredness'
/ɛ/	[ɛ]	voiced half-open front unrounded vocoid; occurs after palatalized consonants and /y/. /gbyɛ̆/ [gbyɛ̆] 'razor', /yē/ [yē] 'it'
	[aʸ]	voiced open central unrounded vocoid with palatalized off-glide; occurs elsewhere. /bʳɛ̆/ [brăʸ] 'grave'

Mada Phonology

/ɛ̃/ [ɛ̃] voiced nasalized half-open front unrounded vocoid; occurs after palatalized consonants. /kʸɛ̃/ [kyɛ̃] 'to look at', /sʸɛ̃/ [ʃɛ̃] 'to wake up'

[ã ʸ] voiced nasalized open central unrounded vocoid with palatalized off-glide; occurs elsewhere. /vɛ̃/ [vã ʸ] 'child'

/ə/ [ɩ] voiced front unrounded vocoid between close and half-close; occurs word final in cv syllables. /kə/ [kɩ] 'house'

[ə] voiced half-close central unrounded vocoid; occurs in cvc and v syllables; /ᴺdər/ [ndər] 'okra'

[ɨ] voiced close central unrounded vocoid; occurs elsewhere. /nənə/ [nɨnɨ] 'to sleep', /məsən/ [mɨsən] 'water'

/a/ [a] voiced open central unrounded vocoid. /là/ [là] 'to help'

/ã/ [ã] voiced nasalized open central unrounded vocoid. /tã/ [tã] 'to chew'

/u/ [ʉ] voiced close central rounded vocoid; occurs following nonvelar and nonlabial consonant articulation. /sū/ [sʉ̄] 'to pour'

[ɨ] voiced close central unrounded vocoid; occurs in data only after voiced labiodental fricative. /vu/ [vɨ] 'to carry away' (In other dialects [u] is /ɨ/ following voiced and voiceless labiodental fricatives (See §10, Buhar [fɨ] 'lungs', but Rija [fū]).

[u] voiced close back rounded vocoid; occurs elsewhere. /wŭ/ [wŭ] 'mosquito'

/ũ/ [ũ] voiced nasalized close back rounded vocoid. /tsʸũ/ [tʃũ] 'forest'

/o/ [õ] voiced nasalized half-close back rounded vocoid; occurs following nasal consonants. /mò/ [mõ̀] 'a lie'

[o] voiced half-close back rounded vocoid; occurs elsewhere. /do/ [do] 'market'

/ɔ/ [ɔ] voiced half-open back rounded vocoid. /fɔ̀/ [fɔ̀] 'to search'

/ɔ̃/ [ɔ̃] voiced nasalized half-open back rounded vocoid. /tɔ̄̃/ [tɔ̄̃] 'ear'

7

Mada Orthography

The following orthography was adopted by the Mada Language Committee, 3 August, 1985.

Consonants

p	=	/p/	m	=	/m/	r	=	/r/
t	=	/t/	n	=	/n/	l	=	/l/
k	=	/k/	ng	=	/ŋ/	h	=	/ʍ/ before /o ɔ u/
kp	=	/kp/	ts	=	/ts/	hw	=	/ʍ/ elsewhere
b	=	/b/	z	=	/dz/	y	=	/y/
d	=	/d/	f	=	/f/	w	=	/w/
g	=	/g/	s	=	/s/			
gb	=	/gb/	v	=	/v/			

m = prenasalization of labials and labial velars
ng = prenasalization of /g/ (that is, ngg for /ᴺg/)
n = prenasalization of other consonants
w = labialization of preceding consonant
y = palatalization of preceding consonant except the following:

        c = /ts^y/   j = /dz^y/
        sh = /s^y/   ny = /ŋ^y/

l = liquid feature before /ə a o ɔ/
r = liquid feature before other vowels

Vowels

i	= /i/	iñ	=	/į/
e	= /e/			
ɛ	= /ɛ/	ɛñ	=	/ɛ̨/
ə	= /ə/			
a	= /a/	añ	=	/ą/
u	= /u/	uñ	=	/ų/
o	= /o/			
ɔ	= /ɔ/	ɔñ	=	/ɔ̨/

Tone diacritics

(unmarked)	=	high tone
¯	=	mid tone
`	=	low tone
ˇ	=	rising tone
^	=	falling tone

8
A Mada Text

A Mada text is presented in this section in a four-line format. The first line is phonetic, the second phonemic, the third orthographic, and the fourth is an English gloss. A fairly free translation is presented usually following blocks of several sentences. The following abbreviations are used for glossing tense-aspect particles: PROG (progressive), CONT (continuative), FUT (future), COND (conditional), and NEG (negative).

[ŋgī̄	là	fɔ	blā̄rạʸ]	[kɩ	sē	tʃɩɲdʒì]
/ᴺgə̄	là	fɔ	Bʳā̄rę̄/	/kə	sē	tsʸiᴺdzʸì/
Nggə̄	là	fɔ	Blā̄reñ.	Kə	sē	cinjì.
I	CONT	search	Blā̄reñ.	he	be	black

[kɩ	la	tè	lɨgā̄	yo]	kɩ	la	tè	kpɩ	yē̄	zɩ̀	yo]
/kə	la	tè	lə̀gā̄	yo/	/kə	la	tè	kpə	yē̄	zə̀	yo/
Kə	la	tè	lə̀gā̄	yo.	Kə	la	tè	kpə	yē̄	zə̀	yo.
he	NEG	has	shirt	not	he	NEG	has	shoes	of	foot	not

[kɩ	sə̄rə	ʈi	kɨnạ̀me]
/kə	sə̄r	ri	kə̄nạ̀me/
Kə	sə̄r	ri	kə̄nàñme.
he	is-black	dirty	much

I am searching for Blā̄reñ. He is black. He has no shirt. He has no shoes. He is very dirty.

[gyī	ma	bī	kɩ	tswē̄	nɨmạ]
/gʸə̄	ma	bə̄	kə	tsʷē̄	nə̄mạ/
Gyə̄	ma	bə̄	kə	tswē̄	nə̄mañ?
you-pl	meet	with	him	place	any

37

```
[sē    bùbwɔ̀   ŋgī    là     te     nɩ     gyī]
/sē    bùbwɔ̀   ᴺgɔ̄    là     te     nə     gyɔ̄/
Sē     bùbwɔ̀   nggɔ̄   là     te     nə     gyɔ̄,
be     pleading I     CONT          make   give   you-pl

[wɔ́    dì     ma     bī     kɩ     ə      ŋkɔ̀]
/wɔ́    də̀     ma     bɔ̄     kə     ə      ᴺkɔ̀/
wɔ́     də̀     ma     bɔ̄     kə     ə      nkɔ̀ñ
anybody COND          meet   with   him    at     road

[nī    kɩ     mą̄     tè     kplā   dì     mą     ɲɛ     dą     tʃų̄]
/nɔ̄    kə     mą̄     tè     kpʳā   də̀     mą     ŋʸɛ    dą     tsʸų̄/
nɔ̄     kə     māñ    tè     kplā   də̀     mañ    nyɛ    dañ    cūñ.
let    hem    then   make   haste  and    then   come   tell   chief

[gyī   gwɔ    ŋgɩ ]
/gyɔ̄   gʷɔ    ᴺgə̀/
Gyɔ̄    gwɔ    nggə̀?
you-pl hear   me
```

Have you met him anywhere? I am pleading with you; if anyone meets him on the road, let him make haste to come and tell the chief. Do you hear me?

```
[blarą̄ʸ  sē    zāʸgyər  ŋgī]   [tī    sē    ų̄ā    me    ə    nə̀ʸ   gyən    tɩ̀]
/Bʳārę   sē    zēgyər   ᴺgɔ̄/   /tɔ̄    sē    yʷā    me    ə    nę̀    gyər    tə̀/
Blārɛñ   sē    zēgyər   nggɔ̄.  Tɔ̄     sē    ywā    me    ə    nèñ    gyər    tə̀.
Blārɛñ   be    brother  my     we     be    two    only  at   belly  mother  ours

[yā    sī     lwè    nə̀ʸ    yē     blarą̄ʸ]  [dì    te     tī    ką     cù̀]
/yā    sə̄     lʷè    nę̄     yɔ̄     Bʳārę/   /də̀    te     tɔ̄    ką     kʸù/
Yā     sə̄     lwè    nēñ    yɔ̄     Blārɛñ,  də̀     te     tɔ̄    kàñ    kyù.
Mother PROG   carry  belly  it     Blārɛñ   and    father ours  take   die

[yā    ɲē     ŋrɩ̀    blarą̄ʸ  dì     ką     cù̀]
/yā    ŋʸɛ    ŋʳį̄    Bʳārę   də̀     ką     kʸù/
Yā     nyɛ̄    ngrìñ  Blārɛñ  də̀     kàñ    kyù,
Mother come  give-birth Blārɛñ  an    take   die
```

Mada Phonology 39

```
[ə  ŋmkpą̄ mē    ŋgī   sī    sē   saʸ   tar   me]
/ə  ᴺkpą̄  mē    ᴺgɔ̄   sɔ̄    sē   sɛ    tar   me/
ə   mkpāñ mē    nggɔ̄  sɔ̄    sē   sɛ    tar   me.
at  time  this  I     PROG  be   year  three only
```

```
[sɔ̰̄  yè  tī  là  sɔ̰  mē]   [tī  la  te  yā  yo]
/sɔ̰̄  yè  tɔ̄  là  sɔ̰  mē/   /tɔ̄  la  te  yā  yo/
Sɔ̀ñ  yè  tɔ̄  là  sɔñ mē,   tɔ̄  la  te  Yā  yo.
sitting which we CONT  sit this  we NEG have Mother not
```

Blārɛñ is my brother. We were the only two from our mother's womb. Mother was carrying Blārɛñ when our father died. Mother died after giving birth to Blārɛñ. I was only three years old at that time. As we are now living, we have no mother.

```
[ŋgī  dą̄   gyī   dą̄   tī   la   te  yā   yo]
/ᴺgɔ̄  dą̄   gʸɔ̄   dą̄   tɔ̄   la   te  yā   yo/
Nggɔ̄ dañ  gyɔ̄  dañ  tɔ̄   la   te  Yā   yo.
I    tell you-pl say  we  NEG  have Mother not
```

```
[ŋgī  tsι   dą̄   gyī   lι   rą̄ʸ   dą̄   sē   ŋgwɔ̃   wɔ   tì]
/ᴺgɔ̄  tsə   dą̄   gʸɔ̄   lə   rę̄    dą̄   sē   ᴺgʷɔ̃   wɔ   tə̀ /
Nggɔ̄ tsə   dañ  gyɔ̄  lə   rɛ̄ñ   dañ  "sē  nggwɔ̃  wɔ   tə̀?"
I    know say  you-pl FUT talk  say   be  who    feed us
```

```
[kι   la   kur      gyī    yo ]
/kə   la   kur      gʸɔ̄    yo/
Kə   la   kur      gyɔ̄    yo?
thought NEG lays-on you-pl not
```

```
[ką̄   gyī   tè   kι   ə   dər   gyī]
/ką̄   gʸɔ̄   tè   kə   ə   dər   gʸɔ̄/
Kāñ   gyɔ̄   tè   kə   ə   dər   gyɔ̄
take  you-pl have thought at heart yours
```

I told you that we have no mother. I know that you will say that: who is it that fed us. Don't you remember? Think about it.

```
[tιte  tī   dą̄   làndār    yè   la   tè   ɲtʃι    yo]
/təte  tɔ̄   dą̄   làᴺdār    yè   la   tè   ᴺtsʸə   yo/
Təte  tɔ̄   dañ  "làndār   yè   la   tè   ncə     yo,
fathers ours said cow     which NEG has tail    not
```

[sē ŋmkparṳ́ wɔ́ là glā yē tʃīŋtʃī]
/sē ᴺkparū wɔ́ là gʳā yē tsʸĪᴺtsʸĪ/
sē Mkparū wɔ́ là glā yē cīncī."
be God   who CONT chase it flies

Our fathers said that "a cow which has no tail, it is God who chases away flies for it."

[ə ŋmkpā̰ mu tī sɪ sɔ̰́ dì ba̰ te tīte̋]
/ə ᴺkpā̰ mu tə̄ sə sɔ̰́ də̀ ba̰ te tə̄tè/
ə mkpā̰ñ mu tə̄ sə sɔ̰́ñ də̀ ba̰ñ te tə̄tè
at time that we PROG sit and those have fathers

[là ba̰ mpɨlā kɨtaɟɔ]
/là ba̰ ᴺpəlā kətagʸɔ/
là bañ mpəlā kətagyɔ.
CONT take food-pieces to-throw

[tī kūlwe kɨ̄ba̰ dì ɥe kɨsɔ̰́ bī kɨ̄kə̄ ə ɲdʒṵ̀]
/tə̄ kūlʷe kə̄ba̰ də̀ yʷe kəsɔ̰́ bə̄ kə̄kə̄ ə ᴺdzʸṵ̀/
Tə̄ kūlwē kə̄ba̰ñ də̀ ywe kəsɔ̰́ñ bə̄ kə̄kə̄ ə njùñ.
we run to-take and go to-sit with fowls at f.shelter

At that time we were sitting and those who had fathers were taking bits of food to toss to us. We ran to take the food and went to sit with the chickens at the chicken shelter.

[blārə̰ʸ gwɔ mī] [də̌r là ŋar ŋgì]
/Bʳār̰ɛ gʷɔ mə̀/ /də̌r là ŋar ᴺgə̀/
Blārɛñ gwɔ mə̀? Də̌r là ngar nggə̀,
Blārɛñ hear able heart CONT break me

[gì là te ŋgì]
/gì là te ᴺgə̀/
gì là te nggə̀,
cry CONT have me

[wī sɔ̰́ ŋmgbiga ə ɥɪ dì glō là tsē wì]
/wə̄ sɔ̰́ ᴺgbəga ə yʷə də̀ gʳō là tsē wə̀/
Wə̄ sɔ̰́ñ mgbəga ə ywə̄ də̀ glō là tsē wə̀?
you sit bush at where and rain CONT beat you

Mada Phonology

[wī sɔ̧ ə tə̄rkì ə ɰι nãr mą̄ ŋų̄ wì]
/wə̄ sɔ̧ ə tə̄rkì ə yʷə nãr mą̄ ŋų̄ wə̀/
Wə̄ sɔñ ə tə̄rkì ə ywə̄ nãr mañ ngūñ wə̀?
you sit at tree at where lightning then kill you

Blārɛñ, do you hear me? My heart is breaking. I feel like weeping. Where are you sitting in the bush where the rain is beating on you? Where are you sitting under a tree where lightning will kill you?

[sē bùbwɔ̀ ŋgī̠ là te nι wì]
/sē bùbʷɔ̀ ᴺgə̄ là te nə wə̀/
Sē bùbwɔ̀ nggə̄ là te nə wə̀.
be pleading I CONT make give you

[kà lι cù̵ cù̵ yē ŋgǎɟù̵ yo]
/kà lə kʸù kʸū yē ᴺgǎgʸū yo/
kà lə kyù kyū yē nggǎgyū yo.
NEG FUT die death of dog not

I beg you; don't die like a dog.

[wī ka ŋgī̠ dɔ̧̀ mų]
/wə̄ ka ᴺgə̄ dɔ̧̀ mų/
Wə̄ ka nggə̄ dɔ̀ñ muñ?
you - me leave why

[blārą̄ʸ ɲē kī]
/Bʳārę̄ ŋʸē kə̄/
Blārɛñ nyē kə̄,
Blārɛñ come home

[blārą̄ʸ ɲē kī]
/Bʳārę̄ ŋʸē kə̄/
Blārɛñ nyē kə̄,
Blārɛñ come home

[ŋgī̠ la te nʉnʉ̀ yo]
/ᴺgə̄ la te nunù yo/
Nggə̄ la te nunù yo.
I NEG have somebody not

Why did you leave me? Blārɛñ, come home. Blārɛñ, come home. I have nobody.

9
The Swadesh 100-Word List

This section lists the first 100 words of the Swadesh word list, as revised in June, 1975, at the University of Ibadan. The data are from Mada, as spoken in Rija, and is transcribed phonemically.

ᴺgə̄	I	sā̧	name
wə̄	thou	ᴺgbərʸa̧	fish
tə̄	we	və̄ᴺtsʸɛ	bird
gʸə̄	ye	kə̀kə̄	chicken
gʸə̀r	one	ᴺgăgʸū	dog
yʷā	two	gūgu	goat
tàr	three	tsʸī̄ᴺtsʸī̄	fly
ᴺlē̠	four	ᴺgbăᴺtə̄	stone
tų	five	kàbu	sand
ᴺgɔ̧	big	màmē	ground
rərē	long	ᴺkɔ̧	road
kukʷɔ	small	gbù	hill
sə̄ᴺba̧	red	rì	sun
kə̄kʳa	white	ʍə	moon
tsʸī̄ᴺdzʸi	black	ᴺtsē	star
gogʳo	hot	bū	night
susù	cool	mə̀sər	water
tsʸʷe	full	yʷɛ̄	egg
sūsʷɛ̀	new	ᴺdzʸō	horn (animal)
tɔ̀	good	ᴺtsʸə, bə̀bè	tail
kukù	dry	ᴺgù	feather
ᴺbə̄	woman	ᴺfù	hair

43

lɔ̄lɔ̧	man	tu	head
nē	person	tɔ̧̄	ear
vɛ̧̄	child	bīsʸi	eye
ᴺvʳe	nose	ŋu̧	kill
ŋʸū	mouth	sʷē	bathe
ŋʸə̄r	tooth	gʸɛ̧	jump
na̧rɛ̧	tongue	dzər	walk
kəyʷɛ ŋʷɔ̧̀	nail (finger)	ŋʸɛ	come
dzə	leg	nə̄	give
ᴺgbərʸu̧	knee	dą̄	say
ŋʷɔ̧	arm/hand	fù	blow
nē	belly	tĕgi	steal
tə̄	neck	gʳo	fire
səsə	breasts	tsə̀ᴺtsē	smoke
də̆r	heart	tùᴺtɔ̧̄	ashes
ᴺgbùᴺgbùr	navel	tərkì	tree
wŭ	roast	bekī	seeds
rē	eat	ᴺgbāᴺvū	leaf
sə̄	drink	ᴺgbərı̧̀	root
ta̧	bite	ᴺgbərı̧̄	rope
mʳe	swallow	ᴺtà̧	skin
ŋʳɛ̧̄	see	na̧	meat
gʷɔ	hear	ᴺtȩ̄	saliva
tsə	know	məgì	blood
te sɔ̧̀	sit down	kuku	bone
kakùr	lie down	məyʷè	fat
nə̀nə̄	sleep	ŋʳi̧	give birth
kʸu	die	rʸù̧	bury

10
A Dialect Comparison of One-Syllable Words

This section presents a comparison of one-syllable words, selected on the basis of maximum number of exact cognates and transcribed phonetically. Gbugyar, Akwanga, and Ungwan Zaria words were not elicited in frames, so no tone is indicated. In Akwanga forms, [x] is a voiceless uvular fricative.

Rija	Gbugyar	Anjagwa	Ancho	Buhar	Akwanga	U. Zaria	English
ɥi̜	ɥi	ɥi̜	ɥi̜	ɥi	ɥi	ɥi	squeeze
rì	ri	rì	rì	ri	ri	ri	ask
ci̜	ci	ci̜	ci̜	ci	ci̜	ci	forehead
ŋri̜	ŋri̜	ŋri̜	ŋri̜	ŋrī̜	ŋri̜	ŋri̜	give birth
ji̜	ji	ji̜	ji̜	ji	ji̜	ji̜	mortar
ɲi̜	ɲi̜	ɲi̜	ɲi̜	ɲi̜	ɲi̜	ɲi̜	elephant
ɥē	ɥe	ɥē	ɥē	ɥē	he	he	go
te	te	te	tʸι	te	te	te	father
tsè	tse	tsè	tsè	tsè	tse	tse	guinea fowl
tswē	tswe	tswē	tswē	tswē	tswə	tso	place
hwι	hwə	hwə	hwə	hwə	hwə	hwa	moon
ɲwę̄	ɲwę	myę̄	myę̄	ɲwę̄	ɲwɛ	mi̜	children
zà̜ʸ	zæ̜	zà̜ʸ	zaʸ	zà̜ʸ	zæ̜	dzę	winnow
ŋrā̜ʸ	ŋre	ŋrę̄	ŋrā̜ʸ	ŋlɛ	ŋræ̜	ŋrę	see
ʃɛ	ʃɛ	ʃɛ	ʃɛ	ʃɛ	sʸɛ	ʃɛ	condiment
ɥā̜ʸ	ɥɛ	ɥā̜ʸ	ɥā̜ʸ	ɥē̜	hæ	hɛ	egg
mā̜ʸ	mɛ	mā̜ʸ	mā̜ʸ	mē̜	mæ	mɛ	build
nā̜ʸ	næ	nā̜ʸ	nā̜ʸ	nā̜ʸ	næ	nɛ	belly
krā̜ʸ	krɛ	krę̄	krā̜ʸ	klɛ	kræ	gbm	finish
mbī	mbə	mbə̄	mbə̄	mbə̄	mbɛ	mba	woman
tsī̜	tsə	tsə̄	tsə̄	tsə̄	tsə	tsa	pot

lʉ	lə	lə̄	lə̄	lə	lə	lɔ	pain
bən	bær	bən	bən	bər	biya	ri	beg
gə̀n	gær	gə̀n	gə̀n	gə̀r	giya	gən	marry
ndə̀r	ndær	ndə̀n	ndə̀n	ndə̀r	ndiya	ndən	okra
ɥà	ɥa	ɥà	ɥà	ɥà	ha	ha	slice
gbǎ	gba	gbǎ	gbǎ	gbā	gba	gba	cock
bwà	bwa	bwà	bwà	bwà	bwa	bwa	pour
ŋā	ŋa	ŋā	ŋā	ŋā	nə	ŋa	return
là	la	là	là	là	la	dzɔ	help
gàr	gar	gàr	gàr	gàr	gɛx	gar	army ant
tsar	tsar	tsar	tsar	tsar	tsəx	tsar	show
gyār	gyar	gyār	gyār	gyār	yəx	ŋar	anger
gbą̄	gbą	gbą̄	gbą̄	gbą̄	gbą	gbą	frog
ɥą̌	ɥą	ɥą̌	ɥą̌	ɥą̌	hą	hą	cover
mą̀	mą	mą̀	mą̀	mą̀	ma	ma	nurse
tą	tą	tą	tą	tą	tą	tą	chew
wù	wu	wû	wû	wù	hu	hu	mosquito
gbù	gbu	gbù	gbù	gbù	gbu	gbo	hill
fū	fu	fū	fū	fɨ	fu	fu	lungs
tʉ	tʉ	tʉ	tʉ	tʉ	tyu	to	head
sʉ̀	sʉ	sʉ̀	sʉ̀	sʉ	sʉ	sʉ	cool
cʉ	cʉ	cʉ	cʉ	cʉ	cʉ	cu	fetch
ɲʉ̄	ɲʉ	ɲʉ̄	ɲʉ̄	ɲʉ̄	ɲʉ	ɲɔ	mouth
ŋʉ	ŋʉ	ŋʉ	ŋu	ŋu	ŋu	ŋo	kill
vʉ̄	vǫ	vǭ	vǭ	vǭ	vǫ	vǫ	seize
cǫ	cǫ	cǫ	cǫ	cǫ	cǫ	cu	forest
mpūr	mpur	mpūr	mpur	mpūr	mpɔx	mpur	fear
tur	tur	tur	tur	tur	tiyʔ	tər	push
gbyǎr	ɟur	ɟūr	gbyār	ɟùr	ʒwɛx	ɥur	bedbug
ŋmgbò	ŋmgbo	ŋmgbò	ŋmgbò	ŋmgbò	ŋmgbo	ŋmgbo	bush yam
tō	to	tō	tō	tō	to	to	burn
dzo	dzo	dzo	dzo	dzo	dzo	dzo	raise
kwǒ	kwɔ	kwǒ	kwǒ	kwǒ	kwɔ	kɔ	bush fowl
dɔ̀	dɔ	dɔ̀	dɔ̀	dɔ̀	dɔ	dɔ	farm
ɟɔ	ɟɔ	ɟɔ	ɟɔ	ɟɔ	yɔ	ɟɔ	call
ŋmgbǫ̌	ŋmgbǫ	ŋmgbǫ̌	ŋmgbǫ̌	ŋmgbǫ̌	ŋmgbǫ	ŋmgbǫ	stomach
ŋgʔ	ŋgʔ	ŋgʔ	ŋgʔ	ŋgʔ	ŋgʔ	ŋgʔ	big
tǭ	tǫ	tǭ	tǭ	tǭ	tǫ	tǫ	ear

Mada Phonology

kpm	kpm	kpm	kpm	kpm	kpm	kpm	kapok tree
kpm	kpm	kpm	kpm	kpm	kpm	kpm	thresh
gbm	gbm	gbm	gbm	gbm	gbm	gbm	canoe

This comparison of one-syllable words is an attempt to show how far an orthography based on Rija speech will represent the speech of other Mada villages. It can be seen that the phonemes of Rija speech will be essentially the same as those of Gbugyar, Anjagwa, Ancho, and Buhar. The phonologies of Akwanga speech and the speech of Ungwan Zaria, on the other hand, are more divergent from the other five villages and from each other.

For Rija, Gbugyar, Anjagwa, Ancho, and Buhar, allophonic conditions are different for front vowels and /ə/; but all the vowel phonemes are the same, except that nasalization of front vowels is more restricted in Gbugyar and Buhar speech. Also, Rija vʉ 'to seize' is phonemically different from the same word in the speech of the other four villages.

Apart from a lower number of cognates with the other speech varieties, Akwanga and Ungwan Zaria apparently also have more significant phonemic differences. Both of these dialects have an [h] in place of [ɥ] before nonhigh vowels. It looks as if this [h] may be an allophone with [ɥ] of a single phoneme in Akwanga and U.Zaria. In the Rija dialect [ɥ] is interpreted as /y^w/, and no [h] occurs before unround vowels.

Rija	Gbugyar	Anjagwa	Ancho	Buhar	Akwanga	U. Zaria	English
ɥi	ɥi	ɥi	ɥi	ɥi	ɥi	ɥi	squeeze
ɥẽ	ɥe	ɥẽ	ɥẽ	ɥẽ	he	he	go
ɥà	ɥa	ɥà	ɥà	ɥà	ha	ha	slice

In Ungwan Zaria speech, /a/ occurs in cv syllables where /ə/ occurs in the other dialects.

Rija	Gbugyar	Anjagwa	Ancho	Buhar	Akwanga	U. Zaria	English
hwɪ	hwə	hwə	hwə	hwə	hwə	hwa	moon
tsĩ	tsə	tsə̃	tsə̃	tsə̃	tsə	tsa	pot

In Akwanga speech, [-əx], [-ɛx] or [-ɔx] occur in place of [-ar] or [-ur]; and [-iya] or [-iyə̃] in place of [-ər] or [-ən].

Rija	Gbugyar	Anjagwa	Ancho	Buhar	Akwanga	U. Zaria	English
gyār	gyar	gyār	gyār	gyār	yəx	ŋar	anger
gàr	gar	gàr	gàr	gàr	gɛx	gar	army ant
mpūr	mpur	mpūr	mpur	mpūr	mpɔx	mpur	fear
gə̀n	gær	gə̀n	gə̀n	gə̀r	giya	gən	marry
tur	tur	tur	tur	tur	tiyʔ	tər	push

References

Greenberg, Joseph H. 1963. The languages of Africa. Bloomington: Indiana University.

Williamson, K. 1971. The Benue-Congo languages and Ijo. In Thomas A. Sebeok (ed), Current Trends in Linguistics 7:245–306. The Hague: Mouton.

Hoffmann, C. F. 1976. List of languages of Nigeria by language families. Ibadan: Department of Linguistics and Nigerian Languages, University of Ibadan.

Grimes, Barbara F. (ed). 1988. Ethnologue: languages of the world. Eleventh edition. Dallas: Summer Institute of Linguistics, Inc.

www.ingramcontent.com/pod-product-compliance
Lightning Source LLC
Chambersburg PA
CBHW051800230426
43670CB00012B/2374